YOUR KNOWLEDGE HAS VALUE

Stefanie Brandl

Aus der Reihe: e-fellows.net stipendiaten-wissen

e-fellows.net (Hrsg.)

Band 1104

Development of a CSR strategy for Toys R Us Germany

GRIN Publishing

Bibliographic information published by the German National Library:

The German National Library lists this publication in the National Bibliography;
detailed bibliographic data are available on the Internet at http://dnb.dnb.de .

Imprint:

Copyright © 2014 GRIN Verlag GmbH
Print and binding: Books on Demand GmbH, Norderstedt Germany
ISBN: 978-3-656-88965-6

This book at GRIN:

http://www.grin.com/en/e-book/288550/development-of-a-csr-strategy-for-toys-r-
us-germany

GRIN - Your knowledge has value

Since its foundation in 1998, GRIN has specialized in publishing academic texts by students, college teachers and other academics as e-book and printed book. The website www.grin.com is an ideal platform for presenting term papers, final papers, scientific essays, dissertations and specialist books.

Visit us on the internet:

http://www.grin.com/

http://www.facebook.com/grincom

http://www.twitter.com/grin_com

Social Responsibility and Ethics in Global Business

Individual Course Project on Corporate Social Responsibility (CSR)

Development of a CSR strategy for Toys"R"Us Germany

Deadline: 12.12.2014

Stefanie Brandl

Content

1. General Information about Toys"R"Us 3

2. Retail Industry in Germany 3
   2.1 General Information about the German Retail Industry 3
   2.2 Most Dominant Stakeholders in the Retail Industry 4
   2.3 Main CSR Issues and the CSR Performance of this Industry 5

3. Development of a CSR Strategy for Toys"R"Us Germany 6
   3.1 Toys"R"Us Germany and Toys"R"Us Inc. in terms of CSR Performance 6
   3.2 CSR Strategy for Toys"R"Us Germany 7
   3.3 The Main Challenges and a Critical Assessment of the Implications of the
       Recommended CSR Strategy 11

4. Conclusion 11

References 12

1. General Information about Toys"R"Us

In 1948 the toy and baby products retailer Toys"R"Us, Inc., headquartered in Wayne, New Jersey, was founded. It offers a wide range of products, including toys, learning aids and children's apparel. Today the company employs 70,000 people in more than 1,700 stores in 37 countries. In Europe, Toys"R"Us, Inc., operates in Austria, France, Germany, Poland, Portugal, Spain, Switzerland and UK (Toys"R"Us, Inc., 2014a). In Germany, Toys"R"Us GmbH (= Toys"R"Us Germany in this paper) was established in 1986 and nowadays ranks with 66 stores, about 1,000 employees and a turnover of EUR 330 million among the biggest toy retailers (Toys"R"Us Germany, 2014a; Bürgel Wirtschaftsinformationen, 2014). In 2014 Toys"R"Us, Inc., launched the strategy "TRU Transformation" to ensure growth and to better implement their mission, bringing joy into lives of their customers. The strategy includes three guiding principles (Easy, Expert and Fair): *"We will be the EASIEST place in the world to find solutions at FAIR prices for kids and babies because we are EXPERTS and understand the joys and challenges of parenting"* (Toys"R"Us, Inc., 2014a). The focus of this paper lies on Toys"R"Us Germany operating in the retail sector.

2. Retail Industry in Germany

2.1 General Information about the German Retail Industry

In 2012 three million people were employed in the German retail business, which is the third largest German economic sector, with sales of EUR 428 billion (Reink, 2014). It can be divided into food (e.g. Aldi), apparel (e.g. H&M), online (e.g. amazon), electronics (e.g. Saturn), furniture retail (e.g. IKEA), drugstores (e.g. dm) and others. Consumers spend 40 percent (EUR 166 billion net sales) of their purchasing power on food while only two percent are spent on toys and hobbies (Bitting, Marschner, Verbeet, 2013; Federal Statistical Office, 2014a). The main costs in the German retail business in 2012 (in percent of the total expenses) included commodities (70 %) and salaries (13 %) (Federal Statistical Office, 2014b) while marketing presented a core investment (HDE, 2014a).

In 2012 approximately 3,400 companies existed in toy retail (Federal Statistical Office, 2014c) whereby most toys were sold in specialized shops (38 %), the Internet (27 %), consumer markets (14 %) and warehouses (10 %) (German Association of Toy and Game Retailers, 2013). Although Germany ranks among the leading toy manufacturer countries in Europe (TIE, 2011a) toys at a value of EUR two billion were imported in 2013 (Federal Statistical Office, 2014d). Thereby 94 percent of the toy products bought from non-EU countries came from Asia, especially China (TIE, 2011b). This is of importance as most of the products being recalled were manufactured in China (Anwar, 2014). Products bought most in Germany are Playmobil (18 %), games and puzzles (16 %), model railways and wheeled toys as well as LEGO (15 % each) (Focus, 2012).

2.2 Most Dominant Stakeholders in the Retail Industry

Corporate social responsibility strategies need to consider the interests of various stakeholders (Sharma, Starik, 2004) but "the vehemence of a stakeholder group does not necessarily signify the importance of an issue – either to the company or to the world" (Porter, Kramer, 2006, p. 4). Therefore it is essential to identify the major stakeholders in the retail sector. Freeman (2010, p. 46) described stakeholders as "any group or individual who can affect or is affected by the achievement of the organization's objectives" and differentiates between primary (communities, customers, employees, suppliers, financiers) and secondary (government, competitors, media, consumer advocate groups and special interest groups) stakeholders (Freeman, Harrison, Wicks, 2007, p. 7). Referring to Buttkus and Neugebauer (2012) the most important stakeholders in retail are 1. Internal stakeholders (e.g. employees), 2. Economical stakeholder (e.g. customers, suppliers), 3. Special interest groups (e.g. environmental organizations) and 4.Communities (e.g. society). They state that consumers are said to be the stakeholders with the highest relevance.

The main CSR issues in the retail business are identified by analyzing the expert opinion of Stefan Genth, managing director of the German Retail Federation (rheinischer-edhv, 2007), as well as by looking at Buttkus and Neugebauer's (2012) description of consumer expectations. In the following, Genth's issues are listed and complemented by Buttkus and Neugebauer's suggestions (in brackets): 1. Responsible product politic and sustainable consumption (regional and sustainable products), 2. Working conditions (sustainable employing politic, trainings), 3. International supply chains (working conditions, wages), 4. Environmental protection and efficient logistics (waste and energy management), 5. Society (openness and transparence, social engagement, open information politics). On top of that, Buttkus and Neugebauer (2012) found that the company philosophy shall be orientated towards social and ecological issues. To conclude, one can say that the five main CSR issues are similar in 2007 and in 2012: 1. Product politic, 2. Working conditions, 3. Supply chain management (SCM), 4. Environment and 5. Society. The European commission (2013) informed that toys are the second most announced product category presenting a risk for health and security (19 % of recalls) after clothes (34 % of recalls), which highlights the relevance of product safety. Research also states that recalls lead to consumer frustrations, negative publicity, loss of brand value and legal actions (Anwar, 2014). Furthermore, the headlines about employee monitoring at e.g. Lidl over the past years show the importance of working conditions.

Concerning the CSR performance, many retail companies still tend to focus on economical issues and little on social and ethical questions. Even today there are no uniform CSR standards and benchmarks. That is why some implement their own initiatives, while others present codes of conducts with a focus on audit of suppliers (Buttkus, Neugebauer, 2012). In Table 1, big retailers selling toys in Germany are listed alongside their CSR activities[1] and stakeholders they address. None of the listed companies (drugstores, warehouses, specialized

---

[1] Due to the limited space available, Table 1 represents a non-exhaustive list of German toy retailers. Kaufhof and Karstadt represent warehouses, Müller rates as a drugstore, mytoys is an online retailer while Lego ranks among manufacturers with own shops whereas Rofu Kinderland and babyone are specialized shops.

shops, manufacturers) has a CSR report although most of them consider CSR, especially the

above mentioned main CSR topics and stakeholders identified in 2.2.

Company	CSR Activities	Stakeholder(s)
Rofu Kinderland	**Yes**, but only in the headquarters (bio cogeneration plant, photovoltaic system) (Rofu Kinderland, n.d.)	Environmental organizations
Babyone	**No** (baby1one, n.d.)	-
Müller	**Yes**, green fleet of trucks, solar energy, recycling, business trips (mueller, n.d.)	Environmental organizations
Kaufhof	**Yes**, sustainability committee, commitment to the European Food Supply Chain Initiative (Galleria Kaufhof, n.d.)	Suppliers
Karstadt	**No** (Karstadt, n.d.)	-
Lego	**Yes**, product safety, environment (SCM, ISO 14001), social responsibility (diversity, safety), human rights (signing global compact), business management, 4 CSR aims: zero product recalls, Top 10 in employee safety, support learning for 101 million children, zero waste (Vestberg, 2012; Vestberg, 2013)	Customers, employees, society environmental organizations, suppliers
Aldi Süd	Yes, customers (product safety), suppliers (Aldi social standards in production), resource management (reducing waste of packaging), operations (carbon footprint), employees (Aldi Management System concerning employees) (Aldi Süd, 2014)	Customers, suppliers, employees, environmental organizations
Mytoys	**Yes**, greenline label for ecological, recyclable and social responsible products (mytoys, 2013)	Customers, environmental organizations

Table 1: CSR Activities of Retailers in Germany

3. Development of a CSR Strategy for Toys"R"Us Germany
3.1 Toys"R"Us Germany and Toys"R"Us Inc. in terms of CSR Performance

Toys"R"Us Germany understands responsibility as meeting the needs of children and their

parents by offering easy accessible markets with enough parking spots, generous and well-

arranged shop space, friendly employees, a vast selection of offers and an outstanding price-

performance ratio (Toys"R"Us Germany, 2014b). This fits with its TRU transformation

strategy mentioned in chapter 1 and indicates that the focus is still on economic and legal

responsibility rather than on ethical and philanthropic goals (Carroll, 1991). Furthermore

Toys"R"Us Germany neither has a CSR report nor a link about "CSR" on their website. Yet

the company mentions two CSR related topics without explicitly naming it CSR: First, by

product safety they mean offering products that comply with European security rules, recalling them in case of safety concerns and giving advice about the safety of toys to their customers. Second, the company supports children's charities, e.g. Ronald McDonald House Charities and SOS Children's Village (Toys"R"Us, Inc., 2014b). Overall, that commitment is rather weak as Toys"R"Us GmbH mainly focuses on calls for donations. Concerning their employees, Toys"R"Us Germany claims to offer "optimal training", but hardly any additional benefits (Toys"R"Us Germany, 2014c).

All in all, one can say that Toys"R"Us GmbH has neither developed a CSR strategy nor do they care a lot about society and environment. The two pillars of engagement, product safety and donations, are small and product safety is even required by law. One gets the impression that the company does not intend to integrate CSR in their daily business as even small initiatives, such as donations, are announced in short press releases instead of publishing them under the children's charities topic on their website. In contrast, the parent company Toys"R"Us, Inc., supports less fortunate kids, military families and the Special Olympics. Moreover, they have volunteering programs and the Geoffrey Fund, which is used to provide monetary assistance to employees affected by personal distress (Toys"R"Us, Inc., 2014b). Additionally, a Toy Guide is made available for customers with disabled children (Toys"R"Us, Inc., 2014c). Toys"R"Us Germany should consider copying some of their parent company's CSR activities.

3.2 CSR Strategy for Toys"R"Us Germany

"No business can solve all of society's problems or bear the cost of doing so. Instead, each company must select issues that intersect with its particular business" (Porter, Kramer, p. 6). Therefore by means of the information collected and provided in the previous chapters, the most relevant social issues for retailers are analyzed. Aldi Süd serves as a role model as it has, in contrast to Toys"R"Us GmbH, a reasonable CSR strategy which emphasizes important stakeholders and addresses main CSR issues in retail. In Table 2 one can see the main CSR issues along with the main stakeholders and customer expectations and how they are currently addressed by Toys"R"Us Germany and Toys"R"Us, Inc., as well as Aldi Süd.

Main CSR Issues	Main Stakeholder	CSR of Toys"R"Us Germany/Inc.	Competitor's CSR (Aldi Süd as best practice)	Customer Expectations
Working Conditions	Employees	Volunteering program[2], Geoffrey fund[2]	Aldi Management System concerning employees	Sustainable employing politic, trainings
Product Politic	Customers	Product safety[2,3], toy guide[2]	Product safety	Regional and sustainable products
SCM	Suppliers		Aldi social standards in production	Working conditions, wages
Environment	Environmental groups		Reducing waste of packaging, carbon foot print	Waste and energy management
Society	Society	Fundraising[2,3]		Openness and transparence, social engagement, open information politics

Table 2: Comparison of the CSR Issue Handling between Toys"R"Us and Aldi Süd (cf. 2.2; 2.3; 3.1)

Working conditions and product politic are the most important issues for Toys"R"Us Germany since every cell is filled with information, which means that the company, their competitors, stakeholders and customers are interested in that topic. SCM, environment and society are categorized second important as there is one empty field in each row. In contrast to Aldi Süd, Toys"R"Us did not yet implement CSR activities to address SCM and environmental issues, although it is of special importance in the retail industry. However, it already does fundraising whereas Aldi Süd did not take up social CSR issues.

To put it in a nutshell, Toys"R"Us Germany has to consider all five CSR issues. Thereby, the focus needs to lay on working conditions, SCM and environment as they did not yet implement any activities in these fields in Germany. Yet, Toys"R"Us needs to extend their engagement when it comes to product politic and society.

To break down the issues the value chain of the company is regarded in Figure 1. It illustrates the inside-out linkages, which are influenced through the company's business operations

---

[2] CSR activity of Toys"R"Us, Inc.
[3] CSR activity of Toys"R"Us Germany

(Porter, Kramer, 2006). The value chain is divided in primary and support activities. Primary activities lead to the physical creation of the product and its sales whereas support activities support primary ones and each other (Porter, 2001).

Issues Concerning Support Activities	
Firm Infrastructure	CSR in Controlling, CSR officer, transparency, code of conduct
Human Resource Management	Training, employee volunteering, working conditions, diversity, health and safety, compensation, layoff policies, work life balance
Technology Development	Testing, material research, stakeholder dialogues, product development and safety, recycling
Procurement	Long-term contracts with suppliers, sustainability criteria, sustainable SCM, natural resources

Issues Concerning Primary Activities		
Logistics and Operations	Marketing and Sales	After-Sales Service
Regional products, emissions, energy and water usage in shops, measuring instruments, hazardous materials, packaging, labor relations	Website, own brands, sustainability labels, consumer information, pricing practices, advertising to children	Recalls, customer satisfaction, disposal

Figure 1: Toys"R"Us Germany's Value Chain and its Social Issues (Porter 1985, own ideas)

Apart from considering the value chain of a company, it is essential to also look at the competitive surrounding when developing a CSR strategy (Porter, Kramer, 2006, pp. 8 – 11). This can be done by using the diamond framework, which allows finding out how local conditions affect the company's ability to compete (Porter, Kramer, 2006, p. 9). However, because of the limited space available, this is not done as part of this paper.

Based on Figure 1, Table 2 and additional research the CSR strategy is now developed for Toys"R"US Germany (Figure 2). As a first step, it is meaningful that Toys"R"Us Germany focuses on working conditions and product politic, since there are already some initiatives (e.g. volunteering program, Geoffrey Fund, Toy Guide) that can be copied from Toys"R"Us, Inc. and can be relatively easy rolled out in Germany. Moreover, the strategy might include conducting surveys and customer dialogues on product safety and customer satisfaction, to better address customer needs, who are the most important stakeholders in retail (2.2). Toys"R"Us should also settle for seals like "spiel gut". This will presumably help to improve customer satisfaction as "consumers are more forgiving of recalls from companies that are otherwise socially responsible and are reputed" (Etayankara, Bapuji, 2009, p. 11). To improve working conditions, Toys"R"Us should also implement the SA 8000 (e.g. concerning working hours according to law, no discrimination) but also complementary offers such as a suggestion system which enables employees to bring forth ideas for improvement and innovation.

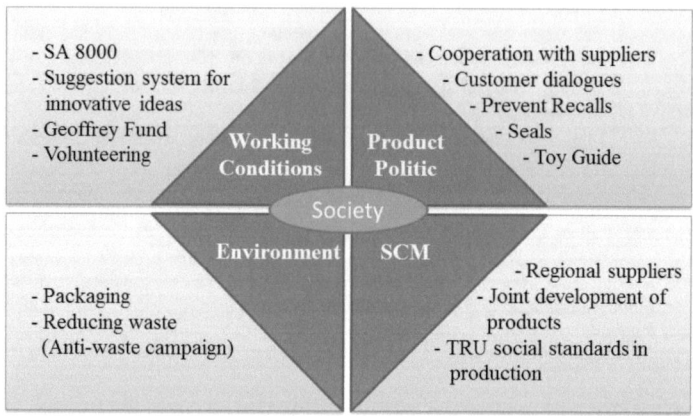

Figure 2: CSR Strategy for Toys"R"Us Germany (own figure)

Subsequently, Toys"R"Us Germany should focus on activities related to SCM and environmental issues to catch up with competitors who did already implement solutions. As found by White and Pomponi (2003), 75 % of all recalls result from shortcomings in product development. That is why Harms, Hansen and Schaltegger (2013) propose to realize the joint development of new products. This seems reasonable for Toys"R"Us as well. Apart from this, the company needs to work closely together with manufacturers and suppliers to establish the basis for good supplier relationships. Together, they can even tackle ecological problems by introducing anti-waste campaigns which might include smaller packaging and recyclable toys with less plastic as well as standards in the supply chain. In this context, Toys"R"Us should also offer transparency of the whole supply chain to customers to better inform and satisfy them. Moreover, it is advisable that Toys"R"Us Germany expands their CSR activities for society especially fundraising for children charities.

Besides implementing different measures, Toys"R"Us Germany is required to open a CSR department with two employees to introduce and monitor the CSR strategy. Thereby, it might be helpful to use sustainability management tools (Hörisch, Johnson, Schaltegger, 2014).

Now as we have seen "[…] CSR can be much more than a cost, a constraint, or a charitable deed – it can be a source of opportunity, innovation, and competitive advantage." (Porter, Kramer, 2006, p. 2; Harms et al, 2013). But there are still some challenges which are discussed in chapter 3.3.

3.3 The Main Challenges and a Critical Assessment of the Implications of the Recommended CSR Strategy

As already stated by Porter (2006, p. 12) "integrating business and social needs takes more than good intentions and strong leadership. It requires adjustments in organization, reporting relationships, and incentives." Especially the adjustment to the organizations· strategy can become difficult because a contradiction of sustainable products can arise with Toys"R"Us Germany's aim to offer a good price-performance ratio. Besides, a CSR strategy implementation is always related to costs for e.g. new employees. Nevertheless it has to be considered that this is only the short-term view. As the CSR activities relate to all parts of the supply chain, difficulties can arise in its implementation since employees do not like the changes, do not have time in their daily business to include the changes or do not have incentives to integrate them. Moreover, it is possible that the CSR strategy does not fit with the company culture. A danger posed by society is that people criticize the strategy as being a greenwashing project or just a copy of other companies' activities in CSR. Furthermore, it might happen that the CSR strategy does not result into monetary benefits, but that the company invests a fortune in communicating the new strategy without getting any advantages.

4. Conclusion

All in all it can be said that CSR is gaining more and more importance and allows advantages in business. Nevertheless "many companies awoke to it only after being surprised by public responses to issues they had not previously thought were part of their business responsibilities" (Porter, Kramer, 2006, p. 2). For that Toys"R"Us Germany should react now to benefit from the opportunities CSR offers as well as from the first mover advantage before more competitors in toy retail start to implement CSR strategies. In the end the investments in e.g. employees or product safety generate advantages and save money.

References

Aldi Süd. (2014). *Responsibility is the Answer*. Retrieved from https://unternehmen.aldi-sued.de/de/verantwortung/verstaendnis/

Anwar, S. T. (2014). Product recalls and product-harm crises: A case of the chainging toy industry. *Competitiveness Review, 24*(3), pp. 190-210.

baby1one. (n.d.). *Babys are our topic*. Retrieved from 1. http://www.babyone.de/is-bin/INTERSHOP.enfinity/WFS/BabyOne-BabyOne_de-Site/de_DE/-/EUR/ViewPage-Start?CatalogName=CompanyPages&PageCategoryName=fachmaerkte

Bitting, H., Marschner, S., & Verbeet, T. (2013). *Counter Retailing Germany 2013: Market study of the 1,000 biggest sales divisions.*

Bürgel Wirtschaftsinformationen. (2014). *Toys "R" Us GmbH: Revenue in 2012*. Retrieved from http://de.statista.com/unternehmen/68284/toys-%2522r%2522-us-gmbh

Buttkus Michael, Neugebauer, Altfried. (2012). *Controlling im Handel: Innovative Ansätze und Praxisbeispiele*: Springer, Gabler Verlag.

Carroll, A. B. (1991). The pyramid of social responsibility: Toward the moral management of organizational stakeholders. *Business Horizons,*

Dr. Jonker Jan, Dipl.-Kfm. Tewes Stefan, Prof. Dr. Stark Wolfgang. (2011). *Corporate Social Responsibility und nachhaltige Entwicklung: Einführung, Strategie und Glossar*. Berlin, Heidelberg: Springer.

Etayankara, M., & Bapuji, H. (2009). Product Recalls: A Review Of Literature. *ASAC,*

European Commission. (2013). *The five most common product categories presenting a risk for health an safety of consumers in Europe 2012*. Retrieved from http://de.statista.com/statistik/daten/studie/258342/umfrage/haeufigste-gemeldete-produktkategorien-die-ein-risiko-fuer-den-verbraucher-darstellen/

Federal Statistical Office. (2014a). *Net turnover in the retail industry by division in Germany in 2012 (in billion Euro)*. Retrieved from http://de.statista.com/statistik/daten/studie/248866/umfrage/umsatz-im-deutschen-einzelhandel-nach-branchen/

Federal Statistical Office. (2014b). *Costs in retail business with share of total costs in Germany 2012*. Retrieved from http://de.statista.com/statistik/daten/studie/261679/umfrage/kostenstruktur-im-einzelhandel-in-deutschland/

Federal Statistical Office. (2014c). *Companies in toy retail business in Germany 2002 - 2012*. Retrieved from http://de.statista.com/statistik/daten/studie/6376/umfrage/unternehmen-im-spielwareneinzelhandel-in-deutschland-seit-2002/

Federal Statistical Office. (2014d). *Foreign Trade of toys in Germany 2005 - 2013 (in billion Euro)*. Retrieved from http://de.statista.com/statistik/daten/studie/258227/umfrage/aussenhandelswert-von-spielwaren-in-deutschland/

Focus. (2012). *Market share from the German toy market measured in revenues 2011*. Retrieved from http://de.statista.com/statistik/daten/studie/214640/umfrage/marktanteile-auf-dem-deutschen-spielwarenmarkt-2011/

Freeman, E. R., Harrison, J. S., & Wicks, A. C. (2007). *Managing for Stakeholders: Survival Reputation and Success. The Business Roundtable Institute for Corporate Ethics Series in Ethics and Leadership*. Yale: Yale University Press.

Freeman, Edward R. et al. (2010). *Stakeholder theory. The state of the art*. New York: Cambridge University Press.

Galeria Kaufhof. (n.d.). *Our company has a tradition of responsibility*. Retrieved from http://www.galeria-kaufhof.de/ueber-uns/verantwortung/verantwortung.html

German Association of Toy and Game Retailers (BVS). (2013). *Distribution of the points of purchase for toys in Germany 2012 - 2013*. Retrieved from http://de.statista.com/statistik/daten/studie/36469/umfrage/kauforte-fuer-spielwaren-in-deutschland/

Harms, D., Hansen, Erik, G., & Schaltegger, S. (2013). Strategies in Sustainable Supply Chain Management: An Empircial Investigation of Large German Companies. *Corporate Social Responsibility and Environmental Management, 20,* 205–2018.

HDE. (2014a). *Core investments in retail business in Germany 2010 - 2014*. Retrieved from http://de.statista.com/statistik/daten/studie/233053/umfrage/interne-investitionen-im-deutschen-handel-im-jahresvergleich/

Hörisch, J., Johnson, Matthew, P., & Schaltegger, S. (2014). Implementation of Sustainability Management and Company Size: A Knowledge-Based View. *Business Strategy and the Environment,*

Karstadt. (n.d.). *Information on Karstadt*. Retrieved from http://www.karstadt.de/on/demandware.store/Sites-Karstadt-Site/de/Page-List?fid=about

mueller. (n.d.). *Typical Müller: Advantage through sustainability*. Retrieved from http://www.mueller.de/unternehmen/nachhaltigkeit.html

mytoys. (2013). *Our mygreenline-Label: Naturally good*. Retrieved from http://www.mytoys.de/mygreenline/KID/de-mt.mk.mygreenline/

Porter, M. E. (2001). *The value chain and competitive advantage. Understanding business: Processes*. London: Barnes, D.

Porter Michael E., Kramer Mark R. (2006). Strategy & Society: The Link Between Competitive Advantage and Corporate Social Respsonsibility. *Havard Business Review, 11.*

Porter, Michael, E. (1985). *Competitive Advantage: Creating and Sustaining Superior Performance*.

Reink, M. (2014). *"Branchenreport Einzelhandel: Stadt und Handel"*. Retrieved from http://www.einzelhandel.de/index.php/publikationen-hde/branchenreport-einzelhandel

rheinischer-edhv. (2007). *HDE-Website with CSR activities in retail business*. Retrieved from http://www.rheinischer-ehdv.de/news_detail.asp?ArticleID=2653

Rofu Kinderland. (n.d.). *Sustainability*. Retrieved from http://www.rofu.de/ueber-rofu/nachhaltigkeit/

Sharma, S., & Starik, M. (2004). *Stakeholders, the Environment and Society: Multiple Perspectives, Emerging Consensus. in Stakeholders, the environment, and society*. Cheltenham, UK: Edward Elgar.

TIE. (2011a). *TIE Facts and Figures 2010*. Retrieved from http://www.tietoy.org/publications/

TIE. (2011b). *Distribution of traditional toy imports from Non-EU-Countries in EU27 countries 2010*. Retrieved from http://de.statista.com/statistik/daten/studie/200234/umfrage/verteilung-der-importe-von-spielwaren-von-nicht-eu-laender-in-die-eu27-laender/

Toys"R"Us, I. (2014a). *About Toys"R"Us, Inc.* Retrieved from http://www.toysrusinc.com/about-us/

Toys"R"Us Germany. (2014a). *Dates & Figures* Retrieved from http://www.de.toysrus.de/ueberuns/daten fakten/

Toys"R"Us Germany. (2014b). *Our company*. Retrieved from http://www.de.toysrus.de/ueberuns/unser-unternehmen/

Toys"R"Us Inc. (2014b). *"R" Employees Give Back*. Retrieved from http://www.toysrusinc.com/charitable-giving/employees-give-back/

Toys"R"Us Inc. (2014c). *Toys "R" Us Toy Guide*. Retrieved from http://www.toysrus.com/shop/index.jsp?categoryId=3261680#section2

Toys"R"Us Germany. (2014c). *Our culture*. Retrieved from http://www.de.toysrus.de/ueberuns/unsere-kultur/

Vestberg, M. (2012). *Responsibility in the Lego Group*. Retrieved from http://aboutus.lego.com/de-de/sustainability

Vestberg, M. (2013). *Performance and Accountability*. Retrieved from http://aboutus.lego.com/de-de/sustainability/performance-and-reporting

White, T., & Pomponi, R. (2003). Gain a competitive edge by preventing recalls. *Quality Progress, 83*(3).